Sun and Sizzle

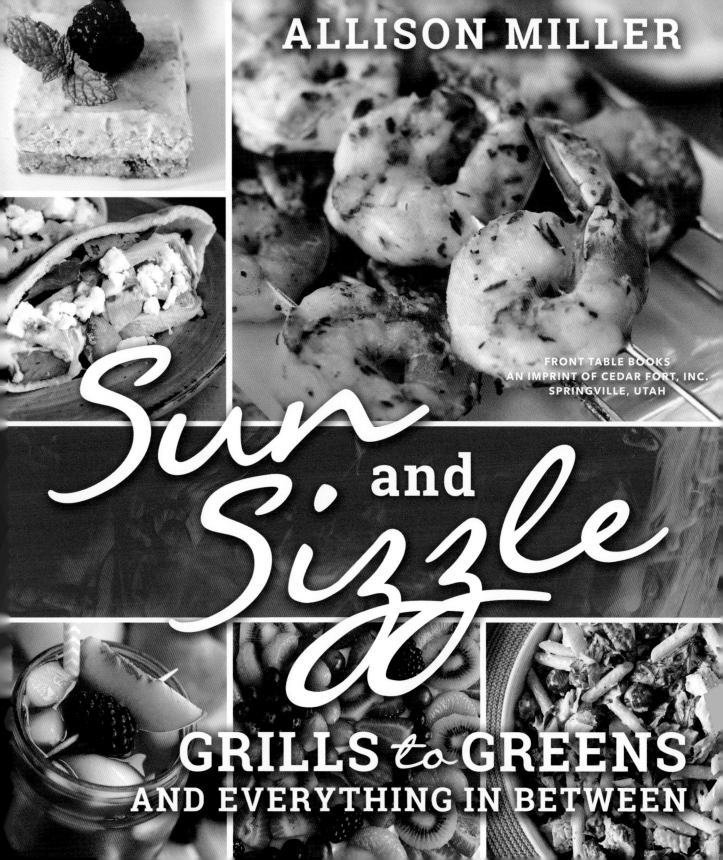

ALLISON MILLER

FRONT TABLE BOOKS
AN IMPRINT OF CEDAR FORT, INC.
SPRINGVILLE, UTAH

Sun and Sizzle

GRILLS to GREENS
AND EVERYTHING IN BETWEEN

ISBN 13: 978-1-4621-1844-1

Published by Front Table Books, an imprint of Cedar Fort, Inc.
2373 W. 700 S., Springville, UT 84663
Distributed by Cedar Fort, Inc., www.cedarfort.com

LIBRARY OF CONGRESS CATALOGING-IN-PUBLICATION DATA
Names: Miller, Allison, 1984- author.
Title: Sun and sizzle : grills to greens and everything in between / Allison
   Miller.
Description: Springville, Utah : Front Table Books, an imprint of Cedar Fort,
   Inc., [2016] | "2016 | Includes index.
Identifiers: LCCN 2015050933 | ISBN 9781462118441 (layflat binding : alk.
   paper)
Subjects: LCSH: Cooking, American. | Quick and easy cooking. | LCGFT:
   Cookbooks.
Classification: LCC TX715 .M63795 2016 | DDC 641.5973--dc23
LC record available at http://lccn.loc.gov/2015050933

Cover design by Rebecca J. Greenwood
Page design by Rebecca J. Greenwood and M. Shaun McMurdie
Cover design © 2016 Cedar Fort, Inc.
Edited by Melissa J. Caldwell

Printed in the United States of America

10 9 8 7 6 5 4 3 2 1

Printed on acid-free paper

To all the fans of *Cupcake Diaries* blog:

This cookbook wouldn't be possible without you,
and I thank you from the bottom of my heart.

This one's for you.

CONTENTS

 1 Entrées

 *29 Side Dishes / Appetizers*

Acknowledgments

A huge thank-you to my wonderful husband, Tyson, who has been my biggest supporter and fan since the beginning. Tyson, I appreciate your endless positivity and the excitement you share about my love of food, photography, and blogging—and the fact that you never complain about any of the crazy stuff. Thank you to my three boys, Brycen, Carter, and Dylan, who have endured many lukewarm meals because Mom wasn't finished taking pictures. Thank you to my neighbors in Syracuse, Utah, for being the ultimate taste testers and welcoming my food into your homes with open arms. I wouldn't be where I am without my parents. Thank you, Mom, for always letting me lick the beaters after baking a yummy treat, adding even more to my love of being in the kitchen. And for letting me stay home from school on occasion just so we could bake together. Thank you, Dad, for instilling a knowledge of determination and perseverance to achieve my goals and dreams. Your guidance and example have helped me many times in my life and during my blogging career. A big thank-you to my sisters, Amber and Amy, for helping me choose the photos for this cookbook and giving me the best advice during the tough times. And thank you, Erika, for introducing me to the wonderful world of cupcakes. I want to thank my family and friends for the endless love, support, and encouragement. I love you all more than I can express.

Introduction

Hello! I am Allison Miller and I welcome you to my first cookbook! I have always loved to cook and bake. Some of my favorite memories as a kid involve helping my mom and grandma in their kitchens, making treats and meals for family and friends. My love of food rose to a new level during the last half of my time at Brigham Young University–Idaho, where I spent my small college student budget on ingredients and baked chocolate chip cookies for roommates and friends on a regular basis. I loved seeing their excitement when I arrived at their apartments with plates of those chocolatey drops of heaven. To this day, I still get messages from college friends about those cookies.

In 2009 I married my husband and joined his amazing family. Our sister-in-law, Erika, had a love for cupcakes and arrived at family activities with the most darling and delicious creations. The cupcake vibe rubbed off on me and I soon found myself making a lot of cupcakes too. Near the end of 2010, I decided I wanted to take this new love of cupcakes and start a recipe blog I appropriately called *Cupcake Diaries*, where I would share fun and easy favorite recipes with family and friends. Especially cupcakes!

My family and friends started sharing my recipes and eventually my little old blog was being seen by people all around the world. Even as my readership continues to grow, I enjoy being genuine to my readers and showing them how this stay-at-home mom cooks and bakes for her family. From the beginning my main focus has been on recipes that can be easily made for a family using common pantry ingredients and little work. My readers can count on quick and easy family-friendly recipes when they visit my blog.

In this cookbook, I've included over fifty recipes for spring and summer, most of which can be made all year long. You will find that these recipes produce amazing and delicious results without a lot of work. For example, the cupcake recipes all start from a cake mix but will look and taste like they came from a bakery. If you've ever had a fear of baking, things are about to change! This cookbook will make things easy for even the most beginner of bakers. As a stay-at-home mom of three young boys, it is a requirement that I make meals they will eat and enjoy. The recipes in this cookbook did not make the cut without the thumbs up from my three toughest critics and biggest fans! You can count on these recipes to not only be delicious but also family friendly and fun.

I am so thankful for all the love and support from not only family and friends but also from my readers. I wouldn't be where I am without all of you. I hope you enjoy my cookbook! And if you're just joining me, come visit me at www.cupcakediariesblog.com!

Love,

Allison Miller

Grilling Tips and Tricks

1. Allow the grill to heat up for 15–20 minutes before throwing uncooked meat on it. This allows the grill to come to a consistent temperature for even and safe cooking.

2. A hot grill is easier to clean. Use a grill brush to clean off charred debris from past use right after it's heated.

3. If you don't have a grill brush, crumple up aluminum foil to the size of an apple and pick it up with tongs. Brush away from you, using the aluminum foil as the brush bristles and the tongs as the brush handle.

4. Have a plate for raw meat and a separate plate for cooked meat, avoiding cross-contamination.

5. Use a spatula or tongs to flip food. Piercing meat with a fork can cause the juices to escape and make the meat dry.

6. Use a grill basket for foods that might fall through the grill rack or are hard to turn over.

7. Create a "safe zone" on the grill by leaving a small area food free and not over the direct heat. This will allow you to move food around as needed and ensure that nothing gets burned.

8. When cooking hamburgers, make an indention in the center of the patty with your thumb. As the meat rises in the center, the patty will stay even and level and won't dome up in the middle.

9. Vegetables are delicious when grilled. To avoid sticking, lightly coat with vegetable oil before placing on the grill.

10. Meat is meant to be flipped just once. After placing it on the grill, allow it to cook for a few minutes and then try pulling it away from the grill. If it sticks, it needs to cook a little longer before flipping.

11. Brush sauces on at the end of cooking so it doesn't burn, as sauce contains sugar and sugar burns easily.

12. After marinating meat, pat it dry so it will sear on the grill and not steam.

13. Remove meat from the grill before it reaches the desired internal temperature. It will continue to cook as it rests.

14. Once meat is off the grill, allow it to rest for about 5 minutes before slicing into it so the juices don't spill out.

Is Your Steak Done?

Steak Temperatures and What They Mean

RARE
- Recommended internal temperature is 125°F.
- Meat is seared and 75 percent red throughout.
- Meat juice is dark red.

MEDIUM-RARE
- Recommended internal temperature is 135°F.
- Meat is seared and 50 percent red throughout.
- Meat juice is light red.

MEDIUM
- Recommended internal temperature is 145°F.
- Meat is seared and center is pink.
- Meat juice is also pink.

MEDIUM-WELL
- Recommended internal temperature is 155°F.
- Meat juice is slightly pink.

WELL
- Recommended internal temperature is 160°F.
- Meat is cooked throughout and brown.
- Meat juice is clear.

Entrées

Grilled Chicken Caesar Sandwiches

Tender grilled chicken sandwiched between crispy bread and layered with creamy Caesar dressing, juicy tomatoes, and crispy lettuce. This easy-to-make sandwich is sure to become a favorite!

Ingredients

2 (8-oz.) **chicken breasts**

½ cup prepared **caesar dressing**

¼ cup grated **Parmesan cheese**

8 slices of your favorite **bread**

romaine lettuce

8 **tomato slices**

Directions

1. Cook the chicken breasts on the grill 3–4 minutes on each side or until done through. Carefully slice each breast into two thinner breasts, making 4. Set aside.

2. Combine caesar dressing and Parmesan cheese in a bowl. Add chicken breasts and coat with the dressing.

3. Broil bread slices for 1 minute with the inside facing up. Place a chicken breast on four of the bread slices. Top with romaine lettuce and two tomato slices. Spread any extra dressing on top bread slice, if desired. Cover sandwich with top bread, slice sandwich, and serve.

Makes 4 sandwiches

Root Beer Pulled Pork Sandwiches

Low and slow is the key to making these tender, juicy pork sandwiches. A perfect recipe to feed a crowd!

Ingredients

1.5–2 lb. **pork roast**

1 envelope **dried onion soup mix**

salt and **pepper**

1 (12-oz.) can **root beer**

2 cups **barbecue sauce**, divided

10 **buns**

Directions

1. Place the pork roast on a work space and sprinkle with dried soup mix; pat all over the roast. Sprinkle generously with salt and pepper and place roast in the slow cooker.

2. In a medium bowl, whisk together root beer and ½ cup barbecue sauce. Pour over the roast.

3. Place the lid on the slow cooker and cook on low heat for 6½–7 hours. Remove the roast from the slow cooker and shred with two forks. Remove all but 1 cup of the juice.

4. Put the shredded pork in the slow cooker with the cup of juice, then add remaining 1½ cups barbecue sauce. Stir into the meat and cook on high for 15–20 minutes to heat the meat. Serve on hamburger buns.

Makes about 10 sandwiches

Aloha Burger

A juicy beef burger piled high with sweet and savory flavors of Hawaii. The juicy pineapple combined with tangy barbecue sauce is a winning combination in this mouthwatering burger.

Ingredients

½ cup **barbecue sauce**

1 (8-oz.) can **sliced pineapple rings**

4 (¼-lb.) **beef patties**

4 slices **Swiss cheese**

4 **hamburger buns**

romaine lettuce

8 slices **bacon**, cooked

Directions

1. Prepare sauce by placing barbecue sauce in a bowl and adding 2 tablespoons of pineapple juice from can of pineapple rings. Stir together and set aside.

2. Grill patties to desired temperature. Add cheese slices and allow to melt before removing patties from the grill.

3. Spread 1 tablespoon sauce on the bottom part of each of the four buns. Cover with lettuce and a patty. Break two bacon slices in half and set on top of patty. Then top with pineapple ring. Spread 1 tablespoon sauce on the inside of the top bun and top the burger and serve.

Makes 4 burgers

Bacon 'n Eggs Burger

A delicious burger with a breakfast twist! It's so good you might not be able to wait until lunch or dinner to make it.

Ingredients

4 (¼-lb.) **beef patties**

4 slices **cheddar cheese**

¼ cup **mayo**

romaine lettuce

4 **hamburger buns**

8 slices **bacon**, cooked

4 **tomato** slices

4 **eggs**, cooked over easy

Directions

1. Grill patties to desired temperature. Add cheese slices and allow to melt before removing patties from the grill.

2. Divide mayo evenly among the four buns and spread over one side. Place lettuce on bottom bun and top with beef patty, followed by two slices of bacon, tomato slice, and egg. Cover with the top bun and serve.

Makes 4 burgers

BBQ Chicken Wraps

Tasty flavors of the Southwest rolled up in a spinach wrap. This wrap is loaded with flavor!

Ingredients

2 **boneless skinless chicken breasts**, grilled and sliced

1 cup **sweet corn**

1 cup **black beans**

1 large **tomato**, sliced

2 cups **lettuce**

1 cup **cheddar cheese**, shredded

1 cup chopped **avocado**

barbecue sauce

ranch dressing

4 **spinach wraps**

Directions

1. Divide chicken among tortillas and place down the middle. Top each with 2 tablespoons corn, 2 tablespoon black beans, tomato slices, ½ cup lettuce, ¼ cup cheese, and ¼ cup avocado.

2. Drizzle with barbecue sauce and ranch dressing, to taste. Fold into a wrap and serve.

Makes 4 wraps

Chicken Teriyaki Pitas

The flavors of a popular Asian chicken dish combine with tangy ranch and sweet pineapple in this mouthwatering wrap. Grab the napkins for this one!

Ingredients

4 **pita pockets**

1 cup **romaine lettuce**

2 **boneless skinless chicken breasts**, grilled and sliced

½ cup **feta cheese** crumbles, divided

½ cup **pineapple chunks**

teriyaki sauce

ranch dressing

Directions

1. Fill each pita pocket with ¼ cup romaine lettuce. Then add half a chicken breast, 2 tablespoons feta cheese crumbles, and 2 tablespoons pineapple slices.

2. Drizzle with teriyaki sauce and ranch dressing, to taste.

Makes 4 pitas

Zucchini Lasagna Rolls

These delicious lasagna rolls are stuffed with fresh zucchini, ricotta, and Parmesan and then topped with chunky marinara sauce. A light alternative with all the flavor of traditional lasagna!

Ingredients

24 oz. **marinara sauce**

3 cloves **garlic**, minced

1 tsp. **olive oil**

2 cups grated **zucchini**, squeezed dry

salt and **pepper**, to taste

1 (15-oz.) container **ricotta cheese**

¾ cup **Parmesan cheese**, grated

1 large **egg**

9 **lasagna noodles**, cooked

1 cup **mozzarella cheese**, shredded

2 Tbsp. **fresh basil**, sliced (optional garnish)

Directions

1. Preheat oven to 350°F. Pour 8 ounces marinara sauce on the bottom of a 9 × 13 baking dish, or enough to cover the bottom.

2. Place garlic and olive oil in a medium skillet and sauté over medium heat for 1 minute. Add zucchini, salt, and pepper, and cook 4–5 minutes, until soft.

3. In a medium bowl, combine the zucchini mixture, ricotta cheese, Parmesan cheese, and egg. Salt and pepper to taste.

4. Pat lasagna noodles dry and lay out on a clean work surface. Take ⅓ cup of ricotta mixture and spread evenly over one noodle. Carefully roll and place seam side down into prepared baking dish. Repeat with remaining noodles.

5. Spoon remaining sauce over lasagna rolls and top each one with 1–2 tablespoons mozzarella cheese. Cover baking dish with foil and bake 40 minutes, or until the inside is heated through and the cheese is melted. Top with fresh basil, if desired.

Makes 9 lasagna rolls

Shrimp, Chicken, and Veggie Pasta

A restaurant-style pasta dish tossed with chicken and shrimp along with bright and fresh summer veggies. Topped with a smooth and hearty cream sauce for a perfect meal.

Ingredients

1 (16-oz.) box **penne pasta**

3 Tbsp. **butter**

20 medium **raw shrimp**, peeled, tail removed, and cleaned

2 **boneless skinless chicken breasts**, grilled and sliced

¾ cup sliced **zucchini**

¾ cup sliced **squash**

1 cup raw **broccoli**

2 cups **heavy cream**

½ cup **Italian blend cheese**

1 tsp. **cayenne pepper**

salt and **pepper**, to taste

Directions

1. Begin cooking pasta according to package directions.

2. Add butter to a large sauté pan and melt over medium heat. Add shrimp, chicken, zucchini, squash, and broccoli. Sauté the mixture until shrimp is cooked and vegetables are soft. Shrimp should be pink.

3. When the pasta is finished cooking, drain the excess water but don't rinse it. Set aside. In the empty pot, add the cream, cheese, and cayenne pepper. Let the cream reduce by half while stirring frequently.

4. Add meat and vegetable mixture to the sauce and stir together. Add pasta and stir together to serve.

Serves 4–6

Bruschetta Chicken

A tasty grilled chicken dish that mimics the classic Italian bruschetta appetizer. Serve with pasta for a complete and satisfying meal!

Ingredients

4 (8-oz.) **chicken breasts**

1 cup **Italian dressing**

2 cups **tomatoes**, diced

1½ tsp. **minced garlic**

2 Tbsp. chopped fresh **basil**

2 Tbsp. **olive oil**

salt and **pepper**, to taste

1 (12-oz.) box **spaghetti**

1½ cups **mozzarella cheese**, shredded

2 Tbsp. **butter**

½ cup **Parmesan cheese**, grated

1 **disposable 9×3 pan**

Directions

1. Place chicken breasts in a gallon ziplock bag with Italian dressing. Seal and place in the fridge for at least 3 hours but no more than 24 hours to marinate.

2. Prepare bruschetta by placing tomatoes, garlic, and basil in a medium bowl. Stir to combine. Drizzle in oil and stir again; add salt and pepper.

3. Use a barbecue grill to cook chicken on medium-high heat. Cook spaghetti according to package directions while chicken is cooking.

4. Turn grill temperature to low once the chicken is cooked. Place disposable pan on grill and place chicken inside. Cover chicken with bruschetta mixture.

5. Sprinkle mozzarella cheese over bruschetta. Close the grill and allow cheese to melt, about 5 minutes. Remove from grill and slice.

6. Toss pasta with butter and place on a platter. Cover with chicken and bruschetta and sprinkle with Parmesan cheese. Serve hot.

Makes 4–6 servings

Grilled Mediterranean Chicken Flatbread Pizzas

Soft flatbread topped with a simple olive oil and garlic sauce and fresh ingredients. A perfectly light meal for a summer evening!

Ingredients

3 Tbsp. **olive oil**

3 **flatbread slices**

Italian seasoning, to taste

3 tsp. **minced garlic**

¾ cup **mozzarella cheese**, shredded

1 cup **spinach leaves**

1 **chicken breast**, grilled and sliced

6 Tbsp. **sun-dried tomatoes**

6 Tbsp. **feta cheese**, crumbled

Directions

1. Assemble pizzas by spreading 1 tablespoon olive oil over each flatbread slice, followed by a pinch of Italian seasoning, 1 teaspoon garlic, ¼ cup mozzarella cheese, ⅓ cup spinach leaves, ⅓ of the chicken slices, 2 tablespoons sun-dried tomatoes, and 2 tablespoons feta cheese.

2. Place pizzas directly on the grill over medium-high heat for 5 minutes, or until mozzarella cheese is melted. Serve hot.

Makes 3 flatbread pizzas

Grilled Lemon Garlic Shrimp Skewers

Perfectly seasoned shrimp topped with a savory garlic butter. A delicious party appetizer!

Ingredients

1 lb. **medium shrimp**, cleaned and deveined

½ cup **butter**, melted

¼ cup **lemon juice**

2 tsp. **garlic powder**

1 tsp. dried **oregano**

1 tsp. dried **thyme**

1 tsp. dried **basil**

salt and **pepper**, to taste

chopped **parsley**, to garnish

Directions

1. Thread shrimp onto skewers and grill over high heat until cooked, about 3–4 minutes on each side.

2. In a small bowl, combine butter, lemon juice, garlic powder, oregano, thyme, basil, and salt and pepper.

3. Baste cooked shrimp with butter mixture and garnish with chopped parsley. Serve immediately.

Makes 20 skewers

Asian Marinated Grilled Shrimp Tacos

A fusion of Thai and Mexican wrapped up into one mouthwatering meal!

Ingredients

1 lb. **shrimp**, cleaned and deveined with tails removed

4 Tbsp. **butter**

4 Tbsp. **soy sauce**

juice of 1 **lime**

2 **green onions**

1 tsp. **ground ginger**

2 tsp. **minced garlic**

4 Tbsp. **sugar**

16 soft **corn tortillas**

2 cups **purple cabbage**, thinly sliced

1 **medium cucumber**, sliced

½ cup **diced pineapple**

⅓ cup **cashews**, chopped

½ cup **cilantro**, to garnish

Directions

1. Place shrimp in a medium bowl and set aside.

2. Combine butter, soy sauce, lime juice, onions, ginger, garlic, and sugar in a sauté pan on medium heat. Let marinade come to a simmer; then remove from heat to cool.

3. Pour marinade over shrimp and cover bowl with plastic wrap. Place in the fridge for 3–5 hours.

4. Thread shrimp onto skewers and place on the grill over high heat until cooked, about 4 minutes per side. Baste the shrimp with extra marinade as it cooks.

5. Prepare tacos by stacking two tortillas and layering with purple cabbage, cucumber, pineapple, cashews, and shrimp. Garnish with cilantro and serve.

Makes 8 tacos

Marinated and Grilled Rib Eye Steaks

A melt-in-your-mouth rib eye cooked to perfection with a 5-minute marinade. Steak night just got easy!

Ingredients

2 Tbsp. **soy sauce**

3 Tbsp. **olive oil**

2 Tbsp. **honey**

2 Tbsp. **Worcestershire sauce**

2 Tbsp. **Dijon mustard**

3 cloves **garlic**, minced

2 Tbsp. **ginger**, minced

2 **rib eye steaks**

Directions

1. Whisk together all marinade ingredients until combined.

2. Place steaks in a plastic ziplock bag and pour marinade over top. Place in the refrigerator for at least 3 hours but no more than 24 hours.

3. Grill steaks over medium-high heat until desired temperature is reached. Serve hot.

Makes 1 cup of marinade

Side Dishes / Appetizers

Mixed Berry Wedge Salad

The berry version of a restaurant classic!

Ingredients

1 **iceberg lettuce wedge**

½ cup **poppy seed dressing**

½ cup **raspberries, blueberries**, and **strawberries**

2 Tbsp. **feta cheese** crumbles

2 Tbsp. **chopped pecans**

Directions

1. Cut a head of iceberg lettuce in half down the center and each of those halves in half to form 4 wedges.

2. Place one of the wedges on a plate and top with dressing. Place the berries on individually so they will stay in place. Add feta and pecans; serve cold.

Makes 1 salad

Chicken Caesar Pasta Salad

Pasta salad meets chicken caesar salad in this tasty side dish! Could also be served as a hearty entree salad.

Ingredients

1 lb. **penne pasta**

2 tsp. **salt**

1 cup **caesar dressing**

¼ tsp. **garlic powder**

1 Tbsp. **lemon juice**

1 head **romaine lettuce**, chopped

10 oz. **grape tomatoes**

½ cup **Parmesan cheese**, shredded

½ tsp. **black pepper**

2 cups **grilled chicken**, diced

Directions

1. Boil pasta in a large pot of water. Add salt and cook according to package directions. Drain completely and rinse under cold water; set aside.

2. In a large bowl, combine caesar dressing, garlic powder, and lemon juice. Add lettuce, tomatoes, Parmesan cheese, pepper, and pasta. Stir until well coated.

3. Add chicken and toss to distribute evenly. Serve immediately.

Makes 1 large salad

Margherita French Bread

Warm and cheesy french bread topped with fresh tomatoes and basil. A great appetizer or meal!

Ingredients

1 loaf **french bread**

½ cup **butter**, softened

3 tsp. **minced garlic**

3 cups **mozzarella cheese**, grated

4 **roma tomatoes**, sliced

½ cup **fresh basil**, sliced

salt and **pepper**

olive oil

Directions

1. Preheat oven to 425°F.

2. Slice bread loaf horizontally through the middle to make two halves. Combine butter and garlic and evenly spread over the inside of each loaf.

3. Sprinkle cheese evenly over both sides. Add tomato slices and basil. Sprinkle with salt and pepper, to taste. Drizzle olive oil over tomatoes.

4. Bake 7–10 minutes, or until cheese is melted.

Makes 2 half loaves

Three Bean Salad

This colorful salad is the perfect side dish for just about any meal. A great salad to bring to picnics, parties, and barbecues!

Ingredients

⅓ cup **apple cider vinegar**

½ cup **sugar**

2 Tbsp. **vegetable oil**

1 tsp. **salt**

¼ tsp. **pepper**

1 clove **garlic**, minced

1 large **shallot**, minced

1 (15.5-oz.) can **green beans**

1 (15.5-oz.) can **dark red kidney beans**

1 (15.5-oz.) can **garbanzo beans**

Directions

1. Whisk vinegar, sugar, oil, salt, pepper, garlic, and shallots. Set aside.

2. Combine beans in a large bowl. Pour sauce over the beans and fold until coated.

3. Cover with plastic wrap and place in the fridge to chill for at least 1 hour to allow flavors to meld. Serve cold.

Makes 5½ cups

Creamy Potatoes and Peas

Potatoes and peas simmered in a creamy sauce. A hearty side dish just like Grandma used to make!

Ingredients

1 lb. **red potatoes**, cleaned and cut

2 cups **carrots**, chopped into chunks

2½ cups **peas**

½ cup **butter**

2 tsp. **salt**

½ cup **flour**

4 cups **milk**

pepper, to taste

Directions

1. Place potatoes and carrots in a pot and cover with water. Bring to a boil and lower heat to simmer. Cook 10 minutes. Add peas and cook 5–7 more minutes.

2. Place butter in a saucepan and melt over medium heat. Add salt and flour. Mix together and then slowly add milk while mixing. Stir and heat to boil; lower heat and cook 1–2 minutes, or until sauce thickens.

3. Drain veggies and place back into the pot. Pour sauce over, and add pepper and more salt, if desired.

Makes 6 cups

Summer Pasta Salad

Every summer get-together needs a pasta salad! This recipe is loaded with flavor and color. Perfect for pairing with Grilled Chicken Caesar Sandwiches.

Ingredients

1 (12-oz.) box **bow tie pasta**

2 cups sliced and quartered **cucumbers**

2 cups grape **tomatoes**, sliced in half

½ lb. **bacon**, cooked and diced

2 cups cubed **colby jack cheese**

1 (16-oz.) bottle **Italian dressing**

Directions

1. Boil water in a large pot and add pasta. Cook according to package directions; drain, rinse, and place in a large bowl.

2. Add cucumbers, tomatoes, bacon, and cheese to pasta. Pour dressing over top and stir to combine. Place in the fridge to chill for at least 1 hour. Serve cold.

Serves 6–8

Baked Parmesan-Herb Zucchini

Oven-roasted zucchini topped with herbs and Parmesan cheese. Perfectly crisp and tender for a delicious summer side dish.

Ingredients

½ cup **Parmesan cheese**, grated

½ tsp. **dried thyme**

½ tsp. **dried oregano**

½ tsp. **dried basil**

¼ tsp. **garlic powder**

14 small **zucchinis**, quartered lengthwise

salt and **pepper**

2 Tbsp. **olive oil**

2 Tbsp. **fresh parsley**, chopped (to garnish)

Directions

1. Preheat oven to 350°F. Coat a cooling rack with nonstick spray and place on a baking sheet.

2. Combine cheese, thyme, oregano, basil, garlic powder, salt, and pepper in a small bowl.

3. Place zucchini on cooling rack and drizzle with oil. Sprinkle cheese mixture over the zucchini. Bake for 15 minutes and then broil for 2–3 minutes until cheese turns a light golden color. Garnish with fresh parsley and serve immediately.

Makes 16 spears

Baked Beans

Classic baked beans slow cooked to perfection. A hearty side dish for a summer meal!

Ingredients

1 lb. **ground beef**

6 slices of **bacon**

2 (15-oz.) cans **pork and beans**

¼ cup **brown sugar**

1 (15-oz.) can **tomato sauce**

1 Tbsp. **mustard**

Directions

1. Preheat oven to 350°F.

2. Cook ground beef in a large sauté pan; set aside. Place bacon slices in the same sauté pan and cook. Pat dry and crumble when cooled.

3. In a large pot, combine pork and beans, brown sugar, ground beef, crumbled bacon, tomato sauce, and mustard. Stir well.

4. Place pot in the oven and bake uncovered for 1 hour. Serve hot.

Serves 6–8

Fresh Salsa

A fresh tomato salsa full of flavor and just the right amount of medium spice and sweetness. Perfect for a summer get-together!

Ingredients

3 **large tomatoes**, diced

½ **white onion**, finely chopped

1 clove garlic, minced

1 (4-oz.) can **chopped green chilies**

juice of 1 lime

½ tsp. **sugar**

½ cup **cilantro**, chopped

1 **jalapeño**, diced with stems and seeds removed

salt and **pepper**, to taste

tortilla chips

Directions

1. In a medium bowl, combine all ingredients but the corn chips and stir together. Add salt and pepper, to taste.

2. Cover and store in the fridge until ready to serve. Serve with tortilla chips.

Makes 3–4 cups

Creamy Corn Dip

Hot and creamy dip with corn, cheese, and bacon. A perfect party appetizer that will be gone in minutes!

Ingredients

6–8 strips of **bacon**

2 (11–15 oz.) cans **whole kernel sweet corn**, drained

1 (8-oz.) pkg. **cream cheese**

1 cup **mozzarella cheese**, shredded

1 tsp. **salt**

dash of **cayenne pepper**

¼ cup **fresh basil**, chopped

tortilla chips

Directions

1. Preheat oven to 400°F.

2. Cook bacon in a sauté pan over medium heat until crispy. Remove and dab with a paper towel.

3. Crumble bacon and place in a small bowl. In a medium bowl, combine corn, cream cheese, mozzarella cheese, salt, cayenne pepper, half the bacon, and half the basil. Place in an 8 × 8 baking dish and bake 20 minutes.

4. Remove from oven and sprinkle with remaining bacon and basil. Serve hot.

Makes 3–4 cups

Antipasto Skewers

Put your antipasto platter on a stick! This is a fresh and easy pickup appetizer for a party that can be made ahead of time.

Ingredients

1 (9-oz.) pkg. **spinach cheese tortellini**

1 (8-oz.) **brick mozzarella cheese**, cut into cubes

1 (6-oz.) can **pitted olives**

1 (10½-oz.) container **cherry tomatoes**

½ cup **prepared pesto**

10–12 **bamboo skewers**

Directions

1. Cook tortellini according to package directions. Rinse and set aside.

2. Thread tortellini, cheese, olives, and tomatoes onto skewers and place on a platter. Spoon desired amount of pesto over each skewer just before serving. Serve cold.

Makes 10–12 skewers

Macaroni Salad

A picnic staple! Make this macaroni salad ahead of time for an easy side dish.

Ingredients

2 cups **elbow macaroni**

½ cup **celery**, chopped

2 Tbsp. **onion**, chopped

1 cup **frozen peas**, cooked

4 Tbsp. **sweet pickle relish**

4 **hard boiled eggs**, chopped

2 tsp. **mustard**

salt and **pepper**, to taste

1 cup **mayo**

Directions

1. Cook macaroni according to package directions; drain, rinse, and then set aside.

2. In a large bowl, combine celery, onion, peas, relish, eggs, mustard, and salt and pepper. Add cooked macaroni and mayo. Stir together and refrigerate. Before serving, stir and add more mayo as needed if the salad dries out. Serve cold.

Serves 6–8

Red Potato Salad

An herbed potato salad without the mayo. This side dish is perfect for a potluck!

Ingredients

12 small **red potatoes**

3 Tbsp. **apple cider vinegar**

1 Tbsp. **olive oil**

1 tsp. **dried thyme**

1 tsp. **dried parsley**

1 Tbsp. **Dijon mustard**

2 tsp. **sugar**

salt and **pepper**, to taste

Directions

1. Cut potatoes into chunks. Place in a pot and fill with water to cover. Add salt and bring to a boil. Cook 15–20 minutes, or until potatoes are tender. Drain and place in a large bowl.

2. Combine apple cider vinegar, olive oil, thyme, parsley, mustard, and sugar in a small bowl. Pour mixture over potatoes and stir together. Add salt and pepper, to taste. Serve hot or cold.

Serves 4–6

Pudding Fruit Salad

You can add your favorite fruits to this easy salad that will complement any meal.

Ingredients

1 (29-oz.) can **peach slices**

1 (20-oz.) can **pineapple chunks**

1 large box **vanilla instant pudding**

1 lb. **strawberries**, quartered

1 **banana**, sliced

½ pint **blueberries**

1 bunch **grapes**

2 Tbsp. **sugar**

Directions

1. Combine peaches, pineapple, and pudding in a large bowl. Do not drain peaches and pineapple. Mix until pudding is dissolved

2. Stir in remaining ingredients; cover and chill. Serve cold.

Serves 10–12

Drinks

Blackberry Peach Lemonade

A fresh peach lemonade with a beautiful puree of juicy blackberries. An incredibly refreshing beverage on a hot day!

Ingredients

3 medium **peaches**, sliced and peeled

1 cup **sugar**

5 cups **water**, divided

1 cup **fresh lemon juice** (about 7 lemons)

1 cup **blackberries** + 1 Tbsp. water, pureed

Directions

1. Place diced peaches, sugar, and 1 cup water in a sauce pan over medium heat. Cook until sugar is dissolved. Mash up peaches with potato masher to break them up. Let mixture simmer until it thickens slightly. Remove from the heat to cool.

2. Strain mixture into a bowl to remove chunks. Add lemon juice and blackberry puree.

3. Carefully pour mixture into a pitcher with remaining 4 cups water. Refrigerate and serve over ice.

Makes 1 pitcher

Melon Punch

A perfectly sweet and refreshing drink with lots of fizz! It's summertime in a glass.

Ingredients

1 **cantaloupe**

1 **watermelon**

1 **honeydew melon**

1 (2-liter) bottle **Sprite**

1 (59-oz.) bottle **Simply Lemonade®**

lemon wedges, to garnish

Directions

1. Ball each of the melons and place fruit on a cookie sheet. Place in the freezer and allow to freeze at least 15 minutes.

2. Put melons in glasses and pour ½ cup Sprite and ½ cup lemonade in each. Garnish with a lemon and serve with a straw.

Makes about 16 cups

Pineapple Orange Smoothie

An easy citrus fruit smoothie with a tropical twist!

Ingredients

4 cups **pineapple chunks**

1½ cup **ice**

¼ cup **orange juice**

⅓ cup **Sprite**

¼ cup **coconut milk**

Directions

1. Place pineapple chunks and ice in a blender; blend to break up.

2. Add orange juice, Sprite, and coconut milk. Continue to blend until smooth. Serve immediately.

Makes 4 smoothies

Sparkling Strawberry Lemonade

Sweet, tangy, and bubbly lemonade with real strawberries. A crispy and fizzy drink for a summer day!

Ingredients

1 small pkg. **frozen strawberries**, thawed and pureed

ice cubes

1 (59-oz.) bottle **Simply Lemonade®**

1 (2-liter) bottle **Sprite**

15 **lemon wedges**, to garnish

Directions

1. Place 2 tablespoons pureed strawberries at the bottom of a glass. Add 3 or 4 whole ice cubes.

2. Pour ½ cup Sprite and ½ cup lemonade over the ice cubes. Garnish with a lemon wedge and serve with a straw.

Makes 15 glasses

Cherry Limeade Cooler

This blended cherry limeade is a fun and refreshing way to quench your thirst. It's easy to make and perfect for a party!

Ingredients

2 cups **ice**

¾–1 (12-oz.) can **frozen limeade concentrate**, depending on preference of tartness

16 oz. prepared **cherry Kool-Aid®**

16 oz. **lemon-lime soda**

lime wedges, to garnish

Directions

1. Place ice cubes in a blender. Add limeade concentrate over top and blend well.

2. Pour prepared cherry Kool-Aid® and lemon-lime soda in the blender. Blend until combined.

3. Pour in glasses and garnish with lime wedges.

Makes 6 glasses

Desserts

Mint Chocolate Chip Ice Cream

Creamy homemade mint ice cream with miniature chocolate chips. A lively and refreshing treat to cool off this summer!

Ingredients

1 pint **whipping cream**

1 (14-oz.) can **sweetened condensed milk**

2 tsp. mint extract, to taste

1 cup **miniature chocolate chips**, plus extra for toppings

5 drops **green food coloring**

Directions

1. Place whipping cream into the bowl of an electric mixer. Beat on high for two minutes, or until stiff peaks form.

2. In a separate bowl, combine sweetened condensed milk, mint extract, chocolate chips, and food coloring. Gently fold in the whipping cream until combined.

3. Pour mixture into a large bread pan (at least 1½ quart). Sprinkle more chocolate chips over top. Cover with plastic wrap and freeze 8 hours or overnight. Serve frozen.

Makes 1½ quarts

Strawberry Ice Cream

Sweet and creamy strawberry ice cream with bits of fresh strawberries throughout. A summertime favorite!

Ingredients

1 pint **heavy whipping cream**

1 (14-oz.) can **sweetened condensed milk**

5 drops **red food coloring**

3 tsp. **strawberry extract**

1 cup **fresh strawberries**, slightly blended

Directions

1. Place whipping cream into the bowl of an electric mixer. Beat on high for two minutes, or until stiff peaks form.

2. In a separate bowl combine sweetened condensed milk, food coloring, strawberry extract, and blended strawberries. Gently fold this mixture in with the whipping cream until combined.

3. Pour mixture into a large bread pan (at least 1½ quart). Cover with plastic wrap and freeze 8 hours or overnight. Serve frozen.

Makes 1½ quarts

Cookies and Cream Ice Cream

A wonderfully creamy, chunky ice cream full of Oreo cookie pieces.

Ingredients

1 pint **heavy whipping cream**

1 (14-oz.) can **sweetened condensed milk**

1 tsp. **pure vanilla extract**

⅓ cup **sugar**

20 **Oreo cookies**, crushed into small pieces

Directions

1. Place whipping cream into the bowl of an electric mixer. Beat on high for two minutes, or until stiff peaks form.

2. In a separate bowl, combine sweetened condensed milk, vanilla extract, sugar, and crushed cookie pieces. Gently fold this mixture in with the whipping cream until combined.

3. Pour mixture into a large bread pan (at least 1½ quart). Cover with plastic wrap and freeze 8 hours or overnight. Serve frozen.

Makes 1½ quarts

S'more Whoopie Pies

Decadent chocolate cookies surrounding a creamy marshmallow buttercream frosting and topped with rich chocolate ganache and crunchy graham cracker crumbs. Tastes just like you're eating a s'more!

Ingredients

COOKIES:

1 box **chocolate cake mix**

6 Tbsp. **butter**, melted and cooled to room temperature

2 **eggs**, whisked

CHOCOLATE GANACHE:

1 cup **heavy cream**

1⅓ cup **semisweet chocolate chips**

pinch of **salt**

crushed **graham crackers** (2 graham cracker sheets)

MARSHMALLOW BUTTERCREAM:

1 cup **butter**, softened but not to room temperature

1½ cups **powdered sugar**

¼–½ tsp. **almond extract**

1 (7-oz.) jar **marshmallow fluff**

Directions

1. Preheat oven to 375°F.

2. Place cake mix in a large bowl; add butter and whisked eggs.

3. Mix dough with wooden spoon or hands until it comes together. Use a cookie scoop to form dough into 1-inch balls. Place on an ungreased cookie sheet and bake for 9–11 minutes. Transfer to a wire rack and allow to cool completely.

4. Prepare ganache by placing heavy cream in a saucepan and chocolate chips in a glass bowl.

5. Bring heavy cream to a boil over medium-high heat, stirring to avoid scalding, and pour over chocolate chips. Allow to cool for 10 minutes.

6. Add salt and whisk together until nice and smooth. Dip the top of 12 cookies in the ganache to coat. Place back on the wire rack and add crushed graham crackers to the dipped part of the cookie.

7. Prepare the marshmallow buttercream by placing the butter in a medium-large bowl. Beat the butter with a mixer until nice and fluffy.

8. Add the powdered sugar about a ½ cup at a time until well combined with the butter. Then add the almond extract. Add marshmallow fluff and mix well.

9. Place the frosting in a 16-oz. frosting bag or a ziplock bag. Cut off the tip of the frosting bag, or one of the corners of the ziplock bag, about ¾ inch up.

10. Press frosting down into the corner of the bag and pipe on the bottom of the remaining 12 cookies. Cover with ganache-dipped cookies to form a sandwich.

11. Allow ganache to cool before serving.

Makes 12 whoopie pies

Strawberry Lemon Cupcakes

The refreshing flavors of strawberry and lemon combined into one delicious cupcake. Just like a tall glass of strawberry lemonade!

Ingredients

CUPCAKES:

1 box **lemon cake mix**

1 cup **buttermilk**

½ cup **vegetable oil**

3 **eggs**

24 **cupcake liners**

STRAWBERRY BUTTERCREAM:

1 cup unsalted **butter**, softened

3 cups **powdered sugar**

1 tsp. **vanilla extract**

½ cup **strawberry preserves**

24 **strawberries**, to garnish

Directions

1. Preheat oven to 375°F.

2. Place cake mix in a large bowl. Add buttermilk, oil, and eggs. Mix with an electric mixer until well combined.

3. Place cupcake liners in muffin pans and fill each liner ⅔ full of batter. Bake 15–17 minutes, or until toothpick inserted comes out clean.

4. Prepare strawberry buttercream by creaming butter in a medium bowl with an electric hand mixer until smooth. Add powdered sugar ½ cup at a time; add vanilla extract and strawberry preserves.

5. Place frosting in a piping bag secured with a frosting tip. Gently squeeze the frosting on each cupcake in a circular motion starting from the outside rim and working your way into the center. Top with a strawberry to garnish.

Makes 24 cupcakes

Root Beer Float Cupcakes

Enjoy the flavors of an old-fashioned root beer float in a cupcake! The creamy root beer buttercream will take you back to your childhood.

Ingredients

CUPCAKES:

1 **vanilla cake mix**

1 cup **root beer**

1 Tbsp. **root beer extract**

½ cup **vegetable oil**

3 large **eggs**

24 **maraschino cherries** with the stems (optional garnish)

24 **cupcake liners**

ROOT BEER BUTTERCREAM:

1 cup **butter**, softened

2 tsp. **root beer extract**

2 Tbsp. **root beer**

3 cups **powdered sugar**

Directions

1. Preheat oven to 375°F.

2. Place cake mix in a large bowl. Add root beer, root beer extract, oil, and eggs. Mix with an electric mixer until well combined.

3. Place cupcake liners in muffin pans and fill each liner ⅔ full of batter. Bake 15–17 minutes, or until toothpick inserted comes out clean.

4. Prepare root beer buttercream by creaming butter in a medium bowl with an electric mixer until smooth. Add root beer extract and 1 Tbsp. root beer; mix again. Add powdered sugar one cup at a time, followed by remaining root beer. Mix until smooth.

5. Pipe frosting onto cupcakes and top with a cherry to serve.

Makes 24 cupcakes

Fruit Pizza

Colorful cookie pizza covered in fresh fruit and a cream cheese frosting. A treat for your eyes and your taste buds!

Ingredients

COOKIE DOUGH:

1 cup **butter**, softened to room temperature

2 cups **sugar**

4 **eggs**

2 tsp. **vanilla extract**

1 tsp. **salt**

½ tsp. **baking soda**

5 cups **flour**

FROSTING:

1 (8-oz.) pkg. **cream cheese**, softened

½ cup **butter**, softened to room temperature

1 tsp. **vanilla extract**

2 cups **powdered sugar**

TOPPINGS:

sliced **fresh fruit**

Directions

1. Preheat oven to 350°F.

2. Beat butter and sugar in a stand mixer on medium speed. Add eggs one at a time; add vanilla extract.

3. In a medium bowl, whisk salt, baking soda, and flour. Slowly add dry mixture to butter mixture until just combined. Place dough in the fridge to chill.

4. Roll dough into a circle to form a big cookie on a round baking stone or pan. Bake 17–20 minutes, or until cookie is a light golden brown on the edges. Let cool and then place in the fridge to chill.

5. Prepare frosting by beating cream cheese and butter until smooth; add vanilla. Add powdered sugar ½ cup at a time.

6. Spread frosting over chilled cookie. Chill again to thicken frosting. Top with fruit slices and serve.

Serves 16–18

Peach Cobbler Cake

Combine fresh peaches and a cake mix for an easy and completely mouthwatering cake!

Ingredients

1 lb. ripe **peaches**, peeled and sliced

1 (12-oz.) can **evaporated milk**

3 **eggs**

1 cup **sugar**

1 Tbsp. **ground cinnamon**

1½ tsp. **ground nutmeg**

1 box **white cake mix**

½ cup **butter**, melted

vanilla ice cream

caramel sauce (optional)

Directions

1. Preheat oven to 350°F. Grease a 9 × 13 pan; set aside.

2. In a medium bowl, combine peaches, milk, eggs, sugar, cinnamon, and nutmeg. Spread mixture into prepared pan and sprinkle cake mix over top. Pour melted butter over the cake mix.

3. Bake for 45–50 minutes, or until peach mixture is bubbly and topping is a light golden brown. Allow cake to cool. Top with ice cream and caramel sauce to serve.

Makes about 16 slices

Peaches and Cream Bars

A fun twist on peach pie! Peach season never tasted so good.

Ingredients

1 cup **flour**

½ cup **quick oats**

½ cup **sugar**

¼ cup **brown sugar**

1 tsp. **cinnamon**

½ cup cold **butter**, cut into pieces

PEACH FILLING:

1 **egg**

½ cup **granulated sugar**

1 Tbsp. **flour**

¼ tsp. **salt**

2 medium **peaches**, peeled and chopped

GLAZE:

½ cup **powdered sugar**

2 tsp. **milk**

½ tsp. **vanilla extract**

Directions

1. Preheat the oven to 375°F. Line an 8 × 8 baking dish with aluminum foil and spray with cooking spray.

2. Whisk flour, oats, both sugars, and cinnamon in the bowl of an electric mixer. Add butter one cube at a time. Mix until pea sized.

3. Set aside 1 cup of the mixture and press the rest into prepared baking dish. Bake 12–15 minutes.

4. Prepare peach filling by whisking egg and sugar until smooth and creamy. Add flour and salt. Fold in peaches.

5. Pour peach filling over hot crust. Sprinkle with remaining 1 cup topping. Bake for another 28–30 minutes, or until golden brown and bubbly. Cool for 30 minutes. Place in the fridge and cool 2 more hours before cutting.

6. Prepare glaze by whisking sugar, milk, and vanilla extract until smooth. Drizzle over each square. Store in the fridge.

Makes 12 bars

Lemon Lush

Smooth layers of tart and sweet lemon and cream over a shortbread cookie crust. A light and refreshing dessert perfect for entertaining!

Ingredients

CRUST:
1 cup **butter**, softened but not to room temperature
2 cups **flour**
¼ cup **sugar**
½ cup **pecans**, finely chopped

CREAM CHEESE LAYER:
2 (8-oz.) packages **cream cheese**
1 cup **powdered sugar**

PUDDING LAYER AND TOPPING:
2 small packages **instant lemon pudding mix**
3½ cups cold **milk**
1 (16-oz) container **Cool Whip**, thawed
lemon zest, to garnish (optional)

Directions

1. Preheat oven to 350°F. Stir together butter, flour, sugar, and chopped pecans in a mixing bowl. A fork works really well to get everything mixed together.

2. Press into a 9 × 13 baking dish and bake 15–20 minutes, or until a light golden brown. Remove from oven and set aside to cool.

3. Beat together cream cheese and sugar until creamy and smooth. Spread over cooled crust.

4. In another mixing bowl, whisk together pudding mix and milk. Allow to sit for 5 minutes to thicken up a little. Spread on top of the cream cheese layer. Cover and place in the fridge for 1 hour.

5. Spread Cool Whip over the pudding layer. Cut into 18–24 pieces (depending on how large or small you cut them) and garnish with fresh lemon zest.

Makes 18–24 servings

Triple Chocolate Zucchini Cupcakes

Perfectly moist zucchini cupcakes with an explosion of chocolate. Topped with a decadent chocolate buttercream frosting for a perfect chocolate lover's dessert!

Ingredients

CAKE:

1 box **chocolate cake mix**

1 tsp. **ground cinnamon**

1 (3.9-oz.) box **instant chocolate pudding**

1 cup **buttermilk**

3 **eggs**

2 cups grated **zucchini**, not drained

24 **cupcake liners**

CHOCOLATE BUTTERCREAM:

1 cup **butter**, softened

4 Tbsp. **milk**

1 tsp. **vanilla extract**

½ cup **cocoa**

3 cups **powdered sugar**

GARNISH:

½ cup **miniature chocolate chips**

Directions

1. Preheat oven to 350°F. Place cupcake liners into muffin cups.

2. Place cake mix in the bowl of an electric stand mixer. Add cinnamon, pudding, buttermilk, and eggs. Mix to combine well; fold in zucchini.

3. Fill cupcake liners ⅔ full and bake for 15–17 minutes. Remove from oven and set cupcakes on cooling rack to cool.

4. Prepare chocolate buttercream by blending butter with an electric hand mixer until smooth. Add 2 tablespoons milk, vanilla extract, and cocoa. Mix well.

5. Add powdered sugar ½ cup at a time. Add remaining milk and blend well.

6. Frost cooled cupcakes and top with miniature chocolate chips.

Makes 24 cupcakes

Raspberry Cheesecake Bars

Smooth raspberry cheesecake over a sweet graham cracker crust. No baking required for this delightful treat!

Ingredients

CRUST:

3 Tbsp. **sugar**

½ cup **butter**, melted

10 **graham crackers**, crushed

CHEESECAKE:

1 pkg. **cream cheese**

1 cup **powdered sugar**

1 cup **whipping cream**

2 cups **raspberries**

½ cup **granulated sugar**

Directions

1. Combine sugar, butter, and crushed graham crackers in a small bowl. Press into an 8 × 8 baking dish and set aside.

2. Beat cream cheese until smooth; add powdered sugar. Pour in whipping cream and beat on high for 3 minutes, or until stiff peaks form.

3. Place raspberries and granulated sugar in a food chopper or food processor and puree. Fold into cream mixture and spread over crust. Place in the freezer for at least 4 hours. Cut into bars and serve frozen.

Makes about 16 bars

No-Bake Marshmallow Peanut Butter Bars

A fast and easy treat held together by marshmallow and butterscotch goodness. No oven required!

Ingredients

3 cups **miniature marshmallows**

2 cups **Rice Krispies® cereal**

1 (11-oz.) pkg. **butterscotch chips**

1 cup creamy **peanut butter**

Directions

1. Line an 8 × 8 baking pan with tin foil and spray lightly with nonstick cooking spray; set aside.

2. Pour marshmallows and cereal into a large bowl. Place butterscotch chips and peanut butter in a microwave safe bowl and heat for 45 seconds. Stir, and heat for 45 seconds more. Then stir until smooth.

3. Pour peanut butter mixture over marshmallows and cereal and stir to coat. Pour in prepared pan. Cover and refrigerate to cool. Cut into bars and serve.

Makes about 16 bars

No-Bake Eclair Cake

This dessert takes about 5 minutes to put together. And it tastes like it came from a bakery! A perfect make-ahead dessert for a crowd.

Ingredients

2 (3.9-oz) boxes **vanilla instant pudding**

3 cups **milk**

8 oz. **Cool Whip**, thawed

1 (14-oz.) box **graham crackers**

CHOCOLATE TOPPING:

⅓ cup **cocoa powder**

3 Tbsp. **milk**

1 cup **sugar**

½ cup **margarine**

1 tsp. **vanilla extract**

Directions

1. Combine pudding and milk in a medium bowl. Stir together to form pudding. Fold in Cool Whip.

2. Layer the bottom of a 9 × 13 baking dish with whole graham crackers. Spread half the pudding mixture over crackers and layer with more graham crackers. Repeat.

3. In a saucepan, combine cocoa powder, milk, and sugar over medium-high heat. Bring to a boil and stir for 1 minute. Remove from heat and add butter and vanilla extract. Stir to melt.

4. Pour chocolate over graham crackers. Cover and refrigerate over night. Serve cold.

Makes a 9 × 13 pan

S'more Cupcakes

Indulge in the flavors of a classic s'more in the form of a delectable chocolate cupcake. No roasting stick required!

Ingredients

24 **cupcake liners**

CUPCAKES:

1 box **chocolate cake mix**

1 cup **buttermilk**

3 **eggs**

½ cup **oil**

CHOCOLATE GANACHE:

1 cup **heavy cream**

1⅓ cups **semisweet chocolate chips**

pinch of **salt**

MARSHMALLOW BUTTERCREAM:

1 cup **butter**, softened but not to room temperature

1½ cups **powdered sugar**

¼–½ tsp. **almond extract**

1 (7-oz.) jar **marshmallow fluff**

2–3 **graham cracker sheets**, roughly to finely chopped

Directions

1. Preheat oven to 350°F.
2. Place cake mix in a mixing bowl; add buttermilk, eggs, and oil, and mix until combined.
3. Place cupcake liners in a muffin tin and fill full with batter. Bake 15–17 minutes. Transfer cupcakes to a wire rack to cool.
4. Prepare ganache by placing heavy cream in a saucepan and chocolate chips in a glass bowl.
5. Bring heavy cream to a boil over medium-high heat, stirring to avoid scalding, and pour over chocolate chips. Allow to cool for 10 minutes.
6. Add salt and whisk together until nice and smooth. Dip the tops of each cupcake up to the liner into the ganache. Place back on the wire rack to cool.
7. Prepare the frosting by placing the butter in a medium/large bowl. Beat the butter with a mixer until nice and fluffy.
8. Add the powdered sugar about a 1/2 cup at a time until well combined with the butter. Then add the almond extract. Add marshmallow fluff and mix well.
9. Place the frosting in a 16-oz. frosting bag or a ziplock bag. Cut off the tip of the frosting bag, or one of the corners of the ziplock bag, about ¾ inch up.
10. Press frosting down into the cut corner of the bag and pipe onto cupcakes in a circular motion. Top with crushed graham cracker.

Makes 24 cupcakes

Chocolate Chip Cookie Dough Cupcakes

Eat a cupcake *and* a chocolate chip cookie with this treat! These cupcakes are stuffed with eggless cookie dough and topped with a cookie dough frosting.

Ingredients

CUPCAKES:
1 box **vanilla cake mix**
1 cup **buttermilk**
3 **eggs**
½ cup **oil**

COOKIE DOUGH CENTER:
1½ cups **butter**, softened
¼ cup **sugar**
½ tsp. **vanilla extract**
2 Tbsp. **milk**
⅛ tsp. **salt**
1½ cups **flour**
½ cup **mini semisweet chocolate chips**

COOKIE DOUGH FROSTING:
1 cup **unsalted butter**, at room temperature
½ cup b**rown sugar**
1 tsp. **vanilla extract**
2–3 Tbsp. **milk**
2½ cups **powdered sugar**
½ tsp. **salt**
½ cup **flour**

GARNISH:
½ cup **mini semisweet chocolate chips**
24 **mini chocolate chip cookies**

Directions

1. Preheat oven to 350°F.
2. Place cake mix in a mixing bowl; add buttermilk, eggs, and oil, and mix until combined.
3. Place cupcake liners in a muffin tin and fill ⅔ full with batter. Bake 15–17 minutes, or until light golden brown on top. Transfer cupcakes to a wire rack to cool.
4. Prepare the cookie dough for the center of the cupcakes by creaming butter and sugar together; add vanilla, milk, and salt. Then add flour. Stir in mini chocolate chips.
5. Using the large side of a frosting tip or something similar, make a hole in each cupcake by pressing it right into the center.
6. Use a spoon to get enough cookie dough that it can be rolled into a little cylinder to fit into the hole in the cupcake. Press the dough right into the cupcake.
7. Use a toothpick to push the cake out of the frosting tip. Tear the top off and press it right on top of the cookie dough to cover it.
8. Prepare the frosting by creaming together butter, brown sugar, vanilla, and 2 tablespoons milk. Slowly add powdered sugar ½ cup at a time to avoid making a huge mess. Then add salt and flour. Add the last tablespoon of milk if you would like a softer frosting.
9. Place the frosting in a 16-oz. frosting bag or a ziplock bag. Cut off the tip of the frosting bag or one of the corners of the ziplock bag, about ¾ inch up. Place a 1M star frosting tip into the hole.
10. Press frosting down into the cut corner of the bag and pipe onto cupcakes in a circular motion. Sprinkle mini semisweet chocolate chips on top, followed by a mini chocolate chip cookie.

Makes 24 cupcakes

Strawberry Crumb Bars

A buttery cookie crust is topped with a sweet strawberry filling and a crunchy crumble and then baked to perfection. A delicious way to use up any extra strawberries!

Ingredients

BARS:

2 cups **flour**

1 cup **sugar**

½ tsp. **salt**

1 cup **cold butter** plus 2 Tbsp., cut into small pieces

¼ cup **brown sugar**

½ cup **quick oats**

1 cup **strawberries**, hulled and diced

½ cup s**trawberry jam or jelly**

½ tsp. **lemon juice**

GLAZE:

1 cup **white chocolate chips**

3 Tbsp. **heavy cream**

1 cup **powdered sugar**

Makes a 9 × 13 pan

Directions

1. Preheat the oven to 375°F. Grease a 9 × 13 pan with nonstick cooking spray and set aside.
2. Combine flour, sugar, and salt in an electric mixer. Turn the mixer on low and add 1 cup cold butter one piece at a time. Continue to mix until everything is well combined.
3. Set 1 cup of this mixture aside. Press the rest of it evenly into the bottom of the greased pan. Bake for 12 minutes, or until edges are slightly browned.
4. While the bottom layer is baking, add brown sugar and quick oats to the remaining dough in the mixer. Add the remaining 2 tablespoons butter and mix until the dough turns clumpy. You can also do this part with your hands.
5. Combine strawberries, jam or jelly, and lemon juice in a small bowl. Use a fork to combine everything and mash up the strawberries, leaving some chunks if desired.
6. Remove cookie crust from the oven and spread strawberry mixture evenly over top. Sprinkle crumble mixture over the strawberry mixture. Bake 20 more minutes. Allow bars to cool before cutting.
7. Prepare glaze by placing white chocolate chips and heavy cream in a microwave save bowl. Microwave for 30 seconds, stir, microwave another 30 seconds, and then stir again until creamy. Heat for longer if chocolate is still chunky. Add powdered sugar and mix well.
8. Place mixture in a small ziplock bag. Cut a small piece off one of the corners. Swirl on the glaze over each bar.

Breakfast / Sweet Breads

Zucchini Pancakes

Breakfast pancakes made with freshly grated zucchini. So easy and the perfect way to sneak in some veggies!

Ingredients

1 cup **sugar**

3 cups **flour**

4 tsp. **baking powder**

1 tsp. **baking soda**

4 **eggs**

1 cup **milk**

½ tsp. **vanilla extract**

2 cups grated **zucchini**, not drained

Directions

1. Whisk together sugar, flour, baking powder, and baking soda. Add eggs, milk, and vanilla; mix well. Fold in zucchini.

2. Pour ¼ cup of batter onto a hot skillet for each pancake. Flip when the top is full of bubbles and cook for one more minute. Serve hot.

Makes about 12 pancakes

Blueberry Muffins with Cinnamon-Sugar Streusel

Soft and fluffy blueberry muffins topped with a cinnamon-sugar streusel for that added crunch. A perfectly sweet breakfast!

Ingredients

MUFFINS:

2 cups **flour**

2 tsp. **baking powder**

¼ tsp. **salt**

½ cup **butter**, at room temperature

1 cup **sugar**

2 **eggs**

1 tsp. **vanilla**

¼ cup **milk**

2 cups **fresh blueberries**

12 **cupcake liners**

STREUSEL:

½ cup **flour**

⅓ cup **granulated sugar**

¼ cup **butter**, melted

½ tsp. **cinnamon**

Directions

1. Preheat oven to 350°F. Line a muffin tin with cupcake liners.

2. Whisk flour, baking powder, and salt in a medium bowl. Cream together butter and sugar with an electric mixer. Add eggs and vanilla. Stir in milk with a wooden spoon.

3. Add dry mixture until just combined. Fold in 1 cup blueberries.

4. Combine streusel ingredients in a small bowl.

5. Fill liners ¾ full of batter. Cover with remaining blueberries and streusel.

6. Bake 18–20 minutes, or until tops are bubbly and light golden brown.

Makes 12 muffins

Churro Waffles

Indulge in breakfast county-fair style with these amazing waffles!

Ingredients

WAFFLES:

2 cups **flour**

⅓ cup **sugar**

4 tsp. **baking powder**

½ tsp. **salt**

2 **eggs**

2 cups **milk**

½ cup **oil**

CHURRO COATING:

1 cup **granulated sugar**

¼ cup **cinnamon**

¼ cup **butter**, melted

Directions

1. Whisk together dry waffle ingredients; set aside.

2. In another bowl, mix together eggs, milk, and oil. Slowly add liquid mixture to dry mixture; mix well.

3. Combine sugar and cinnamon for churro topping in a small bowl. Pour over a dinner plate and spread out.

4. Cook waffles and immediately add butter by dipping or drizzling over the waffles. Place each buttered waffle over the plate of churro coating mixture to coat. Turn over and coat the other side. Serve hot with or without syrup.

Makes 8–10 waffles

Lemon Zucchini Bread

Classic zucchini bread taken to the next level with a pop of citrus flavor. A tasty way to use leftover zucchini!

Ingredients

BREAD:

3 cups **flour**

1 tsp. **salt**

2 tsp. **baking powder**

3 **eggs**

½ cup **oil**

2 cups **sugar**

3 Tbsp. **lemon juice**

½ cup **buttermilk**

zest of 1 lemon

2 cups grated **zucchini**

GLAZE:

1 cup **powdered sugar**

2 Tbsp. **lemon juice**

1 Tbsp. **milk**

Directions

1. Preheat oven to 350°F. Grease a large 9 × 5 bread loaf pan; set aside.

2. Whisk together flour, salt, and baking powder in a medium bowl. In a stand mixer, beat eggs; add oil and sugar. Add lemon juice, buttermilk, and lemon zest.

3. Fold zucchini into the wet mixture and add dry mixture; blend well with the mixer.

4. Pour into greased pan and bake 1 hour.

5. Prepare glaze by combining powdered sugar, lemon juice, and milk in a small bowl. Spoon over warm bread and let set before serving.

Makes one 9 × 5 loaf

Breakfast Casserole Muffins

These muffins are perfect for a family reunion or a quick take-along breakfast. An easy idea for any day of the week!

Ingredients

¾ cup ground **maple pork breakfast sausage**

½ cup **chopped onions**

1½ cup **Bisquick mix**

½ cup **milk**

2 **eggs**

1 tsp **salt**

1 (20-oz.) pkg. **frozen hash browns**

1 cup **cheddar cheese**, shredded

Directions

1. Preheat oven to 375°F. Spray muffin tin with cooking spray.

2. Cook sausage and onion in a large saucepan. Drain and let cool.

3. In a medium bowl, whisk Bisquick, milk, eggs, and salt until blended.

4. Press enough hash browns into each muffin cup to cover bottom and sides and form a cup. Fill each cup about ½–⅔ full with Bisquick mixture. Top with 1–2 tablespoons sausage mixture and cheese.

5. Bake 30 minutes, or until golden brown.

Makes 12 muffins

Blueberry Sweet Rolls

Pillowy soft sweet rolls topped with a sweet lemon glaze and swirled with blueberries. A perfect breakfast roll for any day of the week!

Ingredients

DOUGH:

1 cup **milk**

⅔ cup **sugar**

1½ Tbsp **active dry yeast** (2 packets)

1 stick **butter**, softened

2 large **eggs**

½ tsp. **salt**

4 cups **bread flour**

FILLING:

¼ cup **sugar**

1 tsp. **cornstarch**

1 (10- to 12-oz.) pkg. **frozen blueberries**, still frozen

GLAZE:

1 cup **powdered sugar**

3 Tbsp. **heavy cream**

2 tsp. **lemon juice**

½ tsp. **vanilla**

Directions

1. Heat milk to 95°F in the microwave or in a saucepan. Add milk and sugar to a stand mixer bowl. Stir together with a spoon, then sprinkle yeast over the mixture. Let sit until foamy, about 5 minutes.
2. Add butter, eggs, and salt, and mix with hook attachment on low. Beat in flour and increase speed to medium. Continue beating for 3 minutes, or until a soft dough forms.
3. Increase speed to medium-high and beat dough for 10 minutes. If the dough is too sticky, add a little more flour by the spoonful.
4. Form dough into a ball and place in a greased bowl. Cover with plastic wrap and place in a warm spot to rise for 1 hour, or until double in size.
5. Line the bottom of a 9 × 13 pan with parchment paper and spray with cooking spray. Sprinkle a little flour on the countertop and place the dough ball on top. Roll into a 10 × 24-inch rectangle.
6. Combine sugar and cornstarch in a small bowl. Sprinkle mixture evenly over the dough, leaving about an inch of space along the bottom length of the rectangle. Sprinkle the frozen blueberries over the sugar and cornstarch.
7. Tightly roll dough to form a 24-inch log. Working quickly, cut the dough log in half, then cut each of those two pieces in half, making four separate dough logs. Cut each dough log into 4 evenly sized slices. Place each roll in the prepared pan, cut sides up.
8. Cover the pan with plastic wrap and let rise for 2 hours.
9. Preheat oven to 400°F and bake rolls for 20 minutes, or until golden and bubbly. Cool on a wire rack for 30 minutes before adding glaze.
10. Prepare glaze by whisking together powdered sugar, heavy cream, lemon juice, and vanilla. Drizzle glaze over rolls and serve warm.

Makes 16 sweet rolls

Peanut Butter Waffles with Buttermilk Syrup

Adults and kids alike are going to love these peanut butter waffles. Top with warm buttermilk syrup for a perfect meal!

Ingredients

WAFFLES:

2 cups **flour**

½ cup **sugar**

2¼ tsp. **baking powder**

½ tsp. **baking soda**

1 tsp. **cinnamon**

2 **eggs**

2 cups **milk**

1 cup **creamy peanut butter**

3 Tbsp. **canola oil**

BUTTERMILK SYRUP:

½ cup **butter**

1 cup **sugar**

½ cup **buttermilk**

1 tsp. **Karo syrup**

1 tsp. **baking soda**

1 tsp. **vanilla**

Directions

1. In a medium bowl, whisk together flour, sugar, baking powder, baking soda, and cinnamon.

2. In a separate bowl, combine eggs, milk, peanut butter, and canola oil.

3. Combine wet ingredients with dry ingredients until just combined. Don't overmix. Place in a greased waffle iron and cook.

4. Prepare buttermilk syrup: Bring butter, sugar, buttermilk, and Karo syrup to a boil in a large pan. Remove from heat and stir.

5. Add baking soda and vanilla. The mixture will then fizz to twice the size. Stir occasionally and serve while hot.

Makes 8–10 waffles and 1 cup syrup

Recipe Index

Cooking Measurement Equivalents

CUPS	TABLESPOONS	FLUID OUNCES
⅛ cup	2 Tbsp.	1 fl. oz.
¼ cup	4 Tbsp.	2 fl. oz.
⅓ cup	5 Tbsp. + 1 tsp.	
½ cup	8 Tbsp.	4 fl. oz.
⅔ cup	10 Tbsp. + 2 tsp.	
¾ cup	12 Tbsp.	6 fl. oz.
1 cup	16 Tbsp.	8 fl. oz.

CUPS	FLUID OUNCES	PINTS/QUARTS/GALLONS
1 cup	8 fl. oz.	½ pint
2 cups	16 fl. oz.	1 pint = ½ quart
3 cups	24 fl. oz.	1½ pints
4 cups	32 fl. oz.	2 pints = 1 quart
8 cups	64 fl. oz.	2 quarts = ½ gallon
16 cups	128 fl. oz.	4 quarts = 1 gallon

Other Helpful Equivalents

1 Tbsp.	3 tsp.
8 oz.	½ lb.
16 oz.	1 lb.

Metric Measurement Equivalents

Approximate Weight Equivalents

OUNCES	POUNDS	GRAMS
4 oz.	¼ lb.	113 g
5 oz.		142 g
6 oz.		170 g
8 oz.	½ lb.	227 g
9 oz.		255 g
12 oz.	¾ lb.	340 g
16 oz.	1 lb.	454 g

Approximate Volume Equivalents

CUPS	US FLUID OUNCES	MILLILITERS
⅛ cup	1 fl. oz.	30 ml
¼ cup	2 fl. oz.	59 ml
½ cup	4 fl. oz.	118 ml
¾ cup	6 fl. oz.	177 ml
1 cup	8 fl. oz.	237 ml

Other Helpful Equivalents

½ tsp.	2½ ml
1 tsp.	5 ml
1 Tbsp.	15 ml

About the Author

ALLISON MILLER was born in Salt Lake City, Utah, and moved to Idaho Falls, Idaho, at the ripe old age of two. Her childhood home in Idaho was where her love for food began. She enjoyed helping her mom in the kitchen making all kinds of breads, desserts, and countless family meals. Allison's love for people and photography and her interest in building personal relations with others led her to pursuing a degree in communication at Brigham Young University–Idaho, where she graduated in 2009. Her college experience and love for food came together when she decided to start her food blog, *Cupcake Diaries*. Her recipes have since been featured on multiple websites including *Better Homes and Gardens*, *Fox News*, and *Good Morning America*.

In her spare time, Allison enjoys teaching piano to kids in the neighborhood, traveling, and portrait photography. She and her husband, Tyson, currently reside in Syracuse, Utah, with their three young sons, Brycen, Carter, and Dylan.

SCAN to visit

WWW.CUPCAKEDIARIESBLOG.COM